Endtimes

ALSO BY ALAN WALL:

Poetry
Jacob
Chronicle
Lenses
Gilgamesh
Alexander Pope at Twickenham
Doctor Placebo
Raven

Fiction
Curved Light
Bless the Thief
Silent Conversations
The Lightning Cage
The School of Night
Richard Dadd in Bedlam
China
Sylvie's Riddle

Non-fiction
Writing Fiction
Myth, Metaphor and Science

Endtimes

ALAN WALL

Shearsman Books

Published in the United Kingdom in 2013 by
Shearsman Books Ltd
50 Westons Hill Drive
Emersons Green
BRISTOL BS16 7DF

www.shearsman.com

ISBN 978-1-84861-275-4

First Edition

ACKNOWLEDGEMENTS
Raven first appeared as a chapbook
from Shearsman Books in 2012.

Contents

To Tony Rudolf

Endtimes

Part One

Those Tombs in Ephesus

Dionysius insisted there were the tombs of two Johns in Ephesus, and that is true: I am in both of them. I spent some time on Patmos, then came back here finally. Though written in various cellars of persecution, on an insignificant island, my words commanded attention.

If my Greek is wayward and odd
my Aramaic was a wonder to them all, believe me.
That's how I wrote the gospel
which some redactor cast into the other tongue.
The original lost by Clio's copyists.
Now through the window in the rain
the moon is weeping.
Stars are quicksilver spheres on a black silk windingsheet.

Don't believe the Turin shroud—his was black
woven by the Magdalena
from the anthracite coat of a panther
through countless Gethsemane nights.
She knew her beloved Lord would lie inside it
shortly.

If it's evidence of chronology you need
read these gospels
each authentically carbon-dated
by our grief. Taste
the acrid stink of desolation's cellar.
Penned in that catacomb each hides inside himself.

My words have resurrected him
as he dictated. My work now is
writing his life, tending his mother.

Never a tear from her
since that day on Golgotha.

Should they fall they'd not be
salt water, but atoms, weapons-grade
plutonium, angry enough to eat the whole of Ephesus
leaving it void and smoking.
She keeps a drawer full of resurrection name-tags.

Revise.
Dead man rising in his rags
to stare incredulous into a saviour's face.
And now they say that in the colosseums
lions feed upon his testament.
(Should *Hegemon* be used, I wonder,
in the passages concerning Pilate?)
Beloved disciple
a man hunted and haunted from Palestine to Patmos
half-insane with emblems, symbols,
eschaton's venom.

This world will end one day
he said: never attempt to compute it.
She says almost nothing now.
With the boy at last outside her womb
she knew the end of the world had begun.
Such a calm here finally
sharing our endings in Ephesus.

This afternoon as I wrote
she spent two hours staring
at a dead sparrow on the windowsill.
An invisible hand will surely
come to revive it, but when?
I place a cup of red wine in her palms
she looks down
as if at blood.
Who needs reminding of its colour?

She thinks she might have left some trinkets
on the dark side of the moon—
old CDs; an album of photographs—
a young boy learning the rudiments of carpentry
from his earthly father. Her son, she says,
will collect them for her
once he gets back home and picks up his messages.
The journey turned out longer than we'd thought.

(There is a tradition that, after the crucifixion, the disciple John went to
Ephesus accompanied by Mary. There they both lived to a great age. An
early account held that the author of *The Gospel According to John* was
one and the same as the author of *Revelation*. This has been disputed for
centuries. The texts are so different. But written in different languages,
different genres, different times, might they still claim a single author?
No one actually knows. In any case, you can't always choose your
redactor. History assigns them. One thing we do know: after the
original document was written, it has never ceased to be re-written,
in accordance with each new generation's millenarian expectations.
Apocalyptic visions born at the heart of the Empire.)

Part Two

Patmos, Jerusalem, Rome…

1

In dawnlight this page flashes suddenly
as if the God had settled on it.

First begotten of the dead
the authorities had worked the dark side.

In Rome a senator yawns as news is read out.
All bad. He summons a slave to massage him.
Chi-Rhos and cartoon fishes daubed on catacomb walls.
One more mischievous sect.

And in a cellar on Patmos
a nib scratches over parchment
to uncover the nature of things;
which great machine is thrumming
in the black hole
at the centre of Apocalypse?

Samizdat
scattering electrons from a metal sheet
the vagrant light invaded.

2

Where and when is this light
that has the dark outside it?

At the top of a monochrome hill
surrounding Halifax or Bradford.
Wind and rain between them have darkened
millstone grit till it's black as the times and almost as cold.
Here the chapel stands
translating Gothic weather to wintry redemption.
Upright stones above corpses
bearing inscriptions from the Book of Revelation.
A miscegenation of living and dead
around these parts—
John the Revelator
shines bright enough to penetrate our northern darkness.
Handlooms in cottages fall silent;
still these words carry through millennia.
Whose though?
Give us provenance and taxonomy
you confident sectarians of the glowing faces.

Hölderlin in Tübingen
fastened in his Tower
travels back and forth to Patmos.
Occasional pilgrims stare in at him
spectators at a Bedlam spectacle
torn sheets, wrecked pupa
vacant as the grim northeasterlies.
A sound of wings, lighter than wind, furred and flurried,
not his necessarily.
He is revising *Patmos*,
unintelligible, of course, as was his *Oedipus*.
The darkness of the gods displaying as usual
their *nefas*.

3

The authorities are working the dark side.

Blindfolded men flown over midnight seas
the door held open.
Other heads held under water, over and over
under and
under.
Dogs snarl, inches from your genitals,
laughter drifts from Texas or New Jersey.
What exactly do you understand by the words in your Koran?
Doesn't that Prophet of yours counsel peace and submission?

In Rome a carpenter hides fifteen planks
to make chairs for private sale
tired of the requisitioning
and so many crucifixions.
They might at least let me carve on crosses
emblems of this mighty city
(a wolf suckling the twins)
but no they say
all will be covered in blood.
A redwood forest
in which to hunt meanings with spears.

4

Baffle to enlighten.
Only those with truth inside them
can find a truth outside.
No centurion yet born can understand this.

A dragon coils its Roman tail
round Halifax's fog.
Belches black smoke and methylated spirit
shapeshifting through these shifting weathers.
In its gut the age's sons vomit anathemas.
One has parchment and a nib,
notating the inside of the whale's cathedral
mighty ribwork of the nave.
Latticed roodscreen, Perpendicular arches.
The Great Beast growls Esperanto
from the Aegean to the Pennine hills.
Past swallows future, future erases past.
Some words remain. A lexis of wormwood.
A man may choke on his own vocabulary.
Romans crossed these hills and left paths to prove it
names and dates in stone
statues of silent gods,
Janus grinning in both directions.
Herm cairns on sundry pathways.
Over whaleroads sail prophets
while sunlight brightens on Patmos.
Chrome yellow screams out of blue:
a café painting by Van Gogh.

5

An ivory miniature owned once by Charlemagne
shows John the Divine, his book open before him
a pen in his hand.
To his left the dragon spews fire
to his right on the hill four horsemen stand
awaiting the decisive moment. Its itinerary
clouded for centuries until
re-emergence
falling into the hands
of a German officer in 1940.
When Schmidt was shot through the heart on the Eastern Front
a Russian acquired it along with his Luger
which had jammed exactly when Schmidt had prayed it wouldn't.
Our Red Army man kept Charlemagne's treasure in his pocket
icons being troublesome
under Stalin now as Caesar then.

6

Focus all telescopes on the *eschaton*.

The seven-headed beast of the Apocalypse
on Noah's Ark had a seven-headed wife
to minister unto his needs
which she did most attentively
filling all seven of his mouths with victuals and unction
ensuring that one of their mighty offspring
would be there when most needed
come the end of time.

7

Two hundred yards from Pentecost Chapel
hear trumpets trombones and tubas
sounding the *Introit* to the Second Coming.

In Sunday School today a blacksmith
expounded the Book of Revelation
and when he came to the great white horse he paused
feeling its shod hoof in his hand
a lick of forgeflames on his face.

Colliers and colliers' wives
harmonise the destruction of the planet
in plague and fury, their children immolated
pitlanes tongued with incandescent gas.

Babylon's whore.
Smiling and simpering as dark skies descend.
A hissing of gaslight formulates snaketongue enticements
announcing too
the prelude to a Bible reading.

8

'Jellyfish: little more than organized water.'
A Transcendentalist to Louis Agassiz.
That's how it felt to imperial troops—
organized water in the sea around them.
Some human specimens encountered
in imperial tidal surges
would hang upside down in cages on the streets of Rome.
Sometimes they stare for hours at an albatross
or hunt turtles shy as unicorns.
Laughing even now as they set sail for Britannia
Ultima Thule
where they say the wine's as dirty as the weather.

9

Empedocles gazed down at Etna
before he jumped, thinking:
a philosopher faced with the void
has nothing to add
nothing to say
nothing whatsoever to do
except perhaps this.

Why not save time, tongue and paper?

10

Stanley Kubrick in *Full Metal Jacket*
re-creates Vietnam's Armageddon
on the site of a derelict factory
in South London.

Apocalypse being a moveable feast
even at times a Potemkin village
waiting for Caesar in all his finery to go by
before the deconstruction.

11

After the tribune's visitation
after the day-long meeting in Wannsee
after hearing Caesar rouse the troops
in Rome, Berlin, North Africa
after swearing that the deed be done
though no medal issues forth for this campaign
after bombs dropped over the smoking city
London Dresden Baghdad Hanoi Fallujah
after a regimental silence entered as a sacrament
oaths affirmed
true men of Caesar
the fact-men in tanks, legions
ready at last for another dawn
hunting out the creatures of Apocalypse
scribbling by candlelight in island cellars.

All these we'll question closely.
Telephone Barbie: a good man with questions.
Never takes no for an answer.
Tell him the Leader himself has requested…

12

Natural history even on the inside of Apocalypse
here at the edge of Empire.
Children stumble from dreams
their cries thin reeds rising
out of the waters of sleep.

Birdsong knocks against the window—
that blackbird whose saffron beak
and anthracite feathers
last night warped in the tide.

Still we don't see him.

Mist has swallowed the Welsh hillside.
Giraldus Cambrensis insists
it has a dragon in its belly.
The dragon roaring out these days of tribulation.

Still tomorrow will dawn
clear and sharp as claws in a rock pool.

13

Goebbels affirmed how the greater the lie
the more readily it is believed.

His blond-haired children
Aryan delights
he and Magda poisoned one by one in 1945
secured now from
a world without Hitler in it.

The number of the beast
re-calculates itself each year
always arriving at the same result.
Tattooed on mind not flesh.

14

After Empire comes Weimar.

Whores in gladrags
stepping on to *die Strasse* through expressionist paintings.
Discordant notes from smoky cellars.
Angels with kohl-streaked eyes.
Street uniforms provoke laughter first then riots.
The *Horst Wessel Lied*: its inescapable lament.

A legionary stares in wonder
at such goings-on
lengthy sacrifice incurred
by native liturgies.
Why not simply crucify?
A cheap and rudimentary procedure
the cross re-usable any number of times.

After Weimar
empire once more
this time with upgraded ordnance
better maps
a clear sense of enemies beyond our land lines
and within.

15

Memory's a minefield laid by dissidents.

Forget all that isn't now.
Recover the composure of our blessèd forebears
not oppressed with so much history
accruing each day like guano.
Let their now be ours, the reparations of the present
drained right out of it.

Time contracting, space contracting
the empire soon contained
on a single page
a computer screen
for a Caesar perennially in love with brevity
regal lucidity. Who gives the order
who receives it, standing to attention.

Old tattlers drone on
in city squares
on municipal benches
the names of the glorious dead engraved upon them
invariably saving all their salty praise
for the last emperor but one.

And look there's Osip Mandelstam
on the rainy streets of Petersburg
reciting a poem to the blurred man beside him on the pavement:
lines regarding Caesar
too lethal to write down.

16

In South Maryland tobacco sheds
stand empty
skeletons of an abandoned purpose.
You can hear a curse still if you listen hard
for the white man who once owned these six hundred acres
this rotted wood with its defeated roof.
The howl of a bottle-neck guitar and a harmonica,
ghosts each time the wind comes down the track.

17

It is always the endtime.

The fragment of a turquoise statue
set in a ruined limewashed wall
            in Normandy
one relic to exemplify this mighty enterprise.

Empire turning its cheek to the wind once more.

18

Joseph Mede in *A Key to the Apocalypse* (1627)
dated the end of the world.
Isaac Newton was impressed and went to work himself
employed his knowledge that the lifespan of the locust
measured five months always.

The author of *Principia* reckoned the floor-plan
of the Temple of Solomon provided all necessary info.
Studying this with the aid of mathematics
he devised a plan
for the world's future and its terminus.

He calculated that the end of the world
was any time now.
Empires would inaugurate their teleologies,
counting on this mortmain of statistics
from the Book of Revelation.

19

The empire is explicit, now as then.
Not merely body but soul too
conscripted under oath and under order.
Names listed in the census, *aka* the Book of Life
Caesar's *corpus*
our sacrament announces
Caesar within us
template for our individual and several sacrifice.

Men wept once
hearing the *Horst Wessel Lied*.
Some still do in certain cafés in Nuremburg.

And the sound of marching
either to Tipperary or Poland
announces one time ending
another begun.

(Blake on the streets of London dressed as *sansculotte*
his head a bestiary of a thousand creatures.
An unborn deer was chosen
for its hide to make the finest
vellum bindings, so subtle
in the hands of a manipulator.)

20

Noon. Dead flies. A newspaper
with yesterday's announcements.
The Empire's under threat as usual.
A single lightbulb swings back and forth
above the man strapped to a wooden chair.

His head hangs forward.

The interrogator with the newspaper yawns;
puts it down on the table.

Better get on, he says.
His companion in the corner rises.

Time to rouse the seated fellow
re-apply well-honed techniques to mute recalcitrance.
Empire has a copyright on information
dark stuff secreted in each sleeping brain.

Soon enough we'll wake it out of him
this native son of revelation.

(And though lights drill their faces
24/7
heavy metal blasting
deprivation of the senses
one light remains
peculiarly vivid in its brightness.
Its beam
reconfigured
through Newton's prism
fractures a rainbow.

I saw Eternity the other night...)

21

Only thing we know for sure about empires
is that they all die
losing the confidence that once held sway
over so many tongues in back alleys.
In lands far away of which we know little
they rise up chanting
their creeds, superstitions blossom,
robes soon to be bespattered
with the blood of their oppressors
or vice versa.
While back in London, back in Rome
men behind vast polished desks
sigh at last and grow weary.
The clock's mighty minute hand
amassing its statistics.

22

The lines are all cut to HQ
enemy edging in
when the planes arrive
(co-ordinates half a mile out)
all that strafing and bombing we'd prayed for
hits us not them.

Prayers and curses intermingle.

One of our men calls out to him who is, he says
Alpha and Omega.
The blood pouring out of his neck
means he'll be dead in a few more minutes,
so can find out for himself.

The *acta diurna* will doubtless record
how [*here fill in the number, when known*] brave sons of the empire
donated their lives with composure
to the living word
the living world
of our authority.

And still they edge down to the sea
marching in step
guns on their shoulders touched by the sun
singing Tipperary.
Home again soon as this little
war is won.

23

Patmos, a land of partisans, often deserted.
The summer sun scorches a zone of dust and detritus.

Orestes came here after killing his mother
who had slaughtered his father
with the aid of her toyboy Aegisthus.
The Furies came with him, gregarious and cruel by habit—
still returning on the wind for certain festivals.

Mussolini invaded. A trip down memory lane for some.
Then the Germans took over
less popular in local bars
though not with some local women.
All of them here. Romans, Turks, Germans.
For a while we were colonised only by monks
who rang out angelus bells over white-painted cubes
of stone and plaster
as though it had come already:
the end of all empires.
Except the one that's being minuted
even as we speak.

24

Men have set sail from the Lebanese coast
bearing carvings of cedar
fashioned goddesses, airy spirits
heading for Cornwall at the westernmost
tip of Britannia, and hope to return
with boatloads of tin.

A *Princeps* arrives in a boat filled
with shields, swords, spears
and the Romans who wield them.
In a place set apart on the island
he announces their creed.
No Eichmann is here to take minutes.
Boats come and go
as timetable tides had predicted.
Trade continues
as the persecutions rage.
They harbour up here for wine and provisions
ask who Domitian's been after most recently
and in which houses
women are eyed-up and bought
for what prices, at what rates of exchange
(clean ones, it goes without saying).
I look for truth in their eyes.
Take one cup of wine in silence
return to my cellar and write.

It was Eichmann took the notes that day in Wannsee.
On trial later in Jerusalem
protesting himself a loyal servant of the state
made trains run on time because he had to
whether the midnight cargoes were human or not.
Imperium (for a while at least) bestowed its favours.

As he would say, there's always someone prophesying
in a cellar among rats
on Patmos, in Warsaw
even at the edges of Berlin
with the Führer himself still flourishing.
Before cleansing takes its final turn.

25

The man of discernment stands among ruins at Decapolis
Dresden 1945
Fallujah 2004
or even a dead mill outside Halifax
the windows of its eyes put out
by youthful hunters, nothing left to hunt
(chasing the dragon's tail in smoky corners)
and preaches to the ruined:

Time is ending even as you start to count it.
The kingdom you would cross the globe for
enshrined inside you, all around you.
Split the stick you'll find me there
split the atom you'll find an Etna
grand enough to eat us with flames.
The whale that holds Jonah in its belly
has heated up. No longer gas now
but plasma.

Somewhere towers have started falling
which for traders in the avenues and boulevards below
had seemed for a while
to be heaven.

Split a stick, find me inside
split an atom, find the universe
in a quantum fluctuation
while your father in heaven blinks
a nano-second merely
heaven's duration.

Hiroshima Nagasaki
where we see what happens
when we enter the atom

with all our ingenuity blazing
my brothers and sisters.
My little flock hunting serenity on earth
vague white sheep in mist to whom
I was appointed shepherd.

Your minds weapons-grade. No mist there.
What precisions discovered
in pursuit of your cruelties, Furies.
What pluralities you build, what shining cities
lavishing frail charity
an expertise of centuries regarding ballistics.

Apocalypse: dark powers
working the dark side.
At least see the glow at the heart of the atom
as Empedocles that old atomist did
above the volcano.
For the light shone in darkness
and darkness comprehended it not.

Tell me what shines now
caught gleaming in moonlight
on a man's cheek
in the garden at Gethsemane?

Each salt atom
has a world inside it.
Split it now
to enter heaven.

And remember: all these words
one day
will build one empire
out of another's ruin.

26

And the God was in him, we saw it, heard it.
Touched it, even.
How find words for this?
God, not gods, not the wild creatures
warring in Paradise, impregnating spirits.

A stillness to this light
even as its burns you.

Once one man ascends the clouds
why continue history?

Cape Kennedy's tawdry re-play:
smooth toys, scaffolding, and folds of flame.

All photons he was by then
riddled in light

Uttering its language breath by breath.
Gravity and mass?

Terms non-applicable to post-resurrection phenomena.

27

Goatdrunk, today the Emperor priapic
as a unicorn
needs a virgin lap
to lay his horn in.

Candidates head for the palace
selected according to
eugenic principle, genealogy
breast-size and thigh-configuration.

I sit at a desk by the high window
pen in hand
searching for words adequate to this historical conjuncture.
Not finding them.
His vices: equiponderant;
the precedence between a louse and a flea.

Part Three

Elegiac Days

The emperor always fears assassination.

Domitian my tormentor
spent hours alone each day
spearing flies
with a needle-sharp pen
while my own nib furrowed the parchment
here on Patmos.

Look at him now in his garden.
The seedlings hurrying and swerving around him.
Snowflakes translated to summer.

Always hovered round by priests and priestesses
devotees of one sacred cult or another.
Unchaste vestals he had executed:
Cornelia, Chief-Vestal, buried alive
her lovers clubbed to death
before an avid Roman crowd.
His interest in chastity was not impartial always:
seduced his brother's daughter
who died of the abortion
he forced on her.

Still he valued justice and propriety.
Castration he prohibited then strictly controlled
the price of eunuchs already in the dealers' hands.
A reign full of portents. An eagle (my symbol too)
screeched while embracing his statue at Rome
a raven perched on the Capitol croaking 'All will be well'
but he didn't believe it, preferring 'Nevermore'.
Took writing seriously, gave poetry readings
in his early years, sending to Alexandria
for volumes missing from his library.
Hermogenes forfeited his life through unfortunate allusions

in a historical opus, while his copyists, slaves, were crucified
for exactitude in transmission.
Like Stalin, an affable host
inviting a Palace steward to his bedroom, sharing dinner,
the luxurious couch. Only thing missing
was the vodka.
Come morning the fellow was crucified.

Suspicion now his element.
His daily exercise-gallery lined with
polished moonstone so he could see
any assassin approaching from behind.
Murdered at last by his friends
with his wife's connivance
as stars had predicted. Minerva told him in a dream
how Jupiter disarmed her.

The blade went in repeatedly as later an ice-axe
would hack throughTrotsky's head.
Writing until the very end.

My hand moves over this page
as dawn over Patmos
announces fresh calamities.

My name is John and I am obliged to give witness
to events informed
by history's nightmare, ushering
the day of judgment in—
kingdom come.

I sit here pen in hand
imposing Hebrew forms on Greek constructions
awaiting the knock on the door
in the early hours

sharing such revelation with prophets
already past, and some still to come.

Mandelstam they came for in darkness
who never walked as I did once
along the shores of Galilee
swallowing the sun as though it were
wine in a silver chalice.

Coda

Runemaster gone, leaving behind
curse and blessing cut in stone
weathering our insular anathemas

where footsore scops of chiselled *signum*
once incised these magic characters
leaked poison to wind

according to precise
calendrical malice, mathematical premeditation
séanced from haruspication

glamour chant and invocation
iced sigil, spitting gale
thrashing skies their choristers

waves' carnival
winds' festival
man's funeral.

Safe inside their hearts of oak
on whose bark once
such a runemaster as this would cut

a praise song for *quercus robus*
rings of carboniferous gold
dendrochronology all the way to Adam.

Now in evening light
blazing like an arcade on its boulevard
monks in the scriptorium

limn letters newly brought again from Rome.
A lion couchant
yawns in the margin of Mark's gospel

ready to turn rampant in a single stinking breath
yawn amplified to bellow
swallowing this meek illumination and its logos.

Winds roar unsavioured approval
while our runeman's back in Frisia now
silently chipping flints from silent stone.

Ivory

Definition

Ivory workers in Russia
turned
fossils from Siberia.
No killing needed.
Mother Nature and her white
assassination squads
winter after winter after winter
already providing the antique.

For the purist
only elephant tusk will do
unique modifications of dentine
in transverse sections displaying
in the arc of a circle
decussations forming tiny
curvilinear lozenge-shaped spaces.

But we this day are
latitudinarian; broad-minded
so: walrus narwhal hippopotamus
all white-horned creatures
even unicorn, that evergreen favourite
of libertines and virgins.

Origin of Species

Curious to remark
these chess pieces on a chequered board
were such a short time before
teeth in a walrus mouth.

Cerebretonic strategy and tactics
from last year's dentition
heaving through the salt.

Darwin believed our smile
the vestige of an opened mouth
displaying incisors once
bared to tear cheek and throat.

Elephias Primigenius

has left us now
stepped from that vast wool overcoat
into the ice-creak of extinction.

His ivory remained
to be minutely carved
by Slavic craftsmen here in ill-lit cellars
dreaming vodkas
female flesh
anarchy and revolution.

A copy of *What Is to Be Done?*
lies open on the table
where white dust gathers
tiny mountains
ectoplasm
hardening after evolution's séance.

Circular

Green ivory first cut is mellow.

As the oil dries out
grows whiter, tighter;
shines like a billiard ball
at midnight
ivory moon crossing its verdant nocturn.

On the green baize of Africa
cued memories collide.
Click click
click.

A white man stares along his smooth black barrel.

Report

One ivory cigarette holder
purchased in Jermyn Street
by Sir Edgar Smethwyck, Minister of State
transmits smoke from tobacco
cropped by black hands in Virginia
through the white dentition of our man
sprawled in his leather armchair at the Athenaeum
reading:

Casement's report
dated December 11, 1903
on the Upper Congo
under the reign of Leopold II.

From Matadi thence to Leopoldville
(vainglorious name for any ruler still alive)
so up the Congo to Lolonga River
along the Lopori to Bongandanga
thus to Lake Mantumba.

The cataract region
220 miles in length.

Depopulation through harassment
amputations, execution.
Horrors of the sleeping sickness
even as slaves
ivory
dried fish
are sold today from Stanley Pool.

Larger native canoes largely vanishing
so our Consul reports.

48 goats and 225 fowls
sequestered in a single swoop
houses burned to the ground
although they still hunt hippopotami.

Men shot, their ears cut off
for inadequate deliveries of rubber
even as they labour in their tiny smithies
fashioning bracelets anklets chains.
1000 brass rods or we execute you:
sentries of the La Lulanga Company.

He puts down the report at last
lighting another cigarette.

Names must be deleted
some of the chronicle made vague.

Roger will complain
but comply.

When Smethwyck leaves
he hails a cab
as a ship's arriving in the Pool of London
hold laden with ivory
to be turned and chiselled
within days
in workshops and ateliers
from Bermondsey to Rotherhithe.

Smoke shapes silver curlicues
in a hansom's darkness.
The white ivory holder gleams.
Sir Edgar ponders.

He notes how
in Leopold's dark empire
soldiers must present a hand
for any bullet fired:
evidence of enemy slain.
Thus do countless children
each week
cease to be pentadactylic vertebrates.
Slaughter and oppression
here surely too programmatic.
Human beings, even black ones,
cannot be consigned so cheaply to utility
like piles of bone
bleaching in an equatorial sun.

Questions to be raised in the House.

Marlow's out on deck down there
moored by some murky wharf
spinning his one good yarn
about the heart of darkness.
Kurtz, he says at the narrative's end,
had what appeared to be
'an ivory face'.

Medieval

These diptych leaves
cut from ivory
show John of Patmos
at his revelation.

A dragon's breath:
fluent as a Viking prow.
A woman clothed with sun
wearing a serpent for her sandal.

The Revelator points his quill
to the sky
as though to launch
once more into heaven's blue and white cartography
the bird that flies across each page.
Ink from Elijah's raven
still haunts the mighty.
Lampblack to ivory's mute impeccability
ebony to pale piano keys
sharpening each one.

Pequod

Captain Ahab's ivory leg
fashioned out of polished bone
from a sperm whale's jaw.
Part of him made of the same whiteness
he can't quit hunting.

The ocean will reclaim that severed stump.
Subaquean fossil-makers
pick Ahab clean
of his flesh his dream
that crucifixion in his face
any last hope for his landlocked son.

The cliffs above Whitby
bear an archway
formed from rib-bones of a whale
an opening from one empty space
into another.

Whitby:
where Melville's spirit
spurts through heaven still
spray rising
from a blowing whale.

Flashback

Here is a white with all the colours in it
like Newton's prismed room in Trinity
out of which the rainbow spills
when fractured.

Ivory's
ancient blanched dentition
dances Kandinsky explosions
into dawn.

Hold it in your palm a few moments.
Warms to your flesh.
Soon enough
even here on Jermyn Street
you are back
in the Congo Free State
where you have never been
nor wish to go.

Elegy
(for Nechama)

When I heard she'd died
all I could see all day was the flesh

of her thighs where her white
white skin met the ebony
moss of her mons;
that coastline

(loveliest I ever sank in,
an ocean even warmer than the shore)

we always called the Côte d'Ivoire.

Classified

Buddha made of ivory
many fractures
add to its charm
date unknown
ditto provenance

(at least
six hundred years
one expert reckoned).

Staring at this
nine-inch
god of serenity
with his smiling belly
has kept me sane
these sixty years.

Vendor regrets forced sale.

Raven

Raven and Serpent

The raven noticed the serpent
slithering lithely up the tree's trunk.
A beautiful garden.
One contented couple.

Raven was astounded when serpent spoke.
Now where, he wondered, did the snake learn that?
Are there summer schools these days down there?
Distance learning for winter visitors
even those descended from an unendowed urethra?

Raven's eye shone
bright as a moon if not the sun
when serpent's word
wormed its way down Eve's ear
through her delicate intestines
into her untried womb.

Could I do that? raven asked.
He asked (it should be said) in silence.
Such harmonies as rule here
rule unvocalised.

Noticed for the first time
how tastily the eyes of Adam gleamed
back now from the fields at last
arms filled with red red roses
for the lovely lady.

Emblem

Raven has returned to emblem books.

Of all his second homes
emblem books and bestiaries hold his preference.

There he strolls
admires himself in mirrors of engravings
reads how he never feeds his young
until black feathered quills break through.
Meets unicorn and cockatrice
centaur narwhal and chimera
nods *en passant* to fellow corvids. Never too friendly.

Likes to read about his preference for eyeballs
either on the battlefield
or on the bridge where traitors' heads
get spiked up weekly for his delectation.

And, should he leave the nearby Tower
our kingdom falls in weeks.
Made a home for himself in the word ravenous
despite a host of weeping etymologists forbidding it.
Pruk-pruk, he says to all that. Mr Corvus. Mr Corvax.
Sometimes, while travelling abroad,
he'll answer to Raben or Corbeau
or even Kangee, shape-shifting cousin
from across the seas.

Once long ago his passport said *hraefn*.
and once, when Mighty Corvid issued his command
he fed Elijah who'd been telling
dark truths to kings.

All written out with a black feathered quill
supplied by yours truly.

Wishes they didn't portray him so often
striding over snow
things being seldom black and white like that.

Copernican

Never once doubted that the world was round
while your flat-footed granddaddy Neanderthals
took care they didn't look over the edge of things
and fall.

The world designed to fit exactly in each eyeball
ours or yours.

Something we ponder frequently enough
while chewing.

Migration

For centuries we stared from cliffs
at the itching
heaving
terrible flesh of the sea.

Then moved inland
for good.

Festivities

Once a year come Christmas
distant relatives arrive to tell their tales.
Here's *garrulus gladarius*
flashing his boutique colours
and his bling.

Then *pica pica*, blue and black and white
as though to wake a dozing farmer.

For ourselves we like the sable:
stay funereal, darkly-suited.

Appropriate avian ushers from on high
saving our *pruk-pruks* till later
when the real festivities begin.

For the record

Not one of us (not one)
ever uttered the word Nevermore.

And a gift for mimicry
not unlike your own
would mean
we never would repeat it
over and over like that.

One black-feathered bird perched inside
the troubled head of Edgar Allan Poe
had taken to drink.

A Peaceable Kingdom

Our relative the jackdaw, a friend from the east
likes the roofs of your castles
the more antique the better.
For ourselves we prefer mountains.
Virtuous men love mountains
wise men the sea—so I have heard.
In which case we are virtuous
our monogamy as unrelenting
as our plumage.

As for diet
needs must when the devil drives.
Today so far one mouse one shrew
one nesting infant from a neighbour's copse
beetles grubs
locusts and moths.

Keeping our heads cocked
for any sound of distant battle.
But you have grown pacific of late
hoping perhaps to starve us out with kindness.

Operatic

Sometimes at night I dream
trees and skies are one
and a derelict camper van
in the field below
has a god growing wise inside it.
He swallows winds
the way his antique fathers did in Egypt once.
Now and then
borrows the voice of a nearby television aerial.
An occasional rat climbs inside him to pray.
His words intermittent, lucid, terrible.
Prepare my dark-eyed friends
a mighty feast, he says.
And remember Belshazzar.

Winds sometimes shake these trees
a shudder loud enough to get life started
like a chorus from Wagner
where one world or another is dying.

Evensong

Once we all gathered on your cathedral roof
to hear you sing of kings
kings and saviours
the journey down and the journey upwards
men with wings and luminous hair
who fly in bearing messages from heaven
for blind old prophets crooked in their inglenooks.

We thought it wonderful.
If ravens could cry believe me we'd have wept.
Pruk-pruk, we chorused from our separate gargoyles.
Pruk
Pruk
Pruk.

Mimicry

Looking at your first
Howard Hughes contraptions
made us *pruk* so merrily
we pecked one another's feathers in jest.
They'll never get up here with us.

Closer to the dinosaurs ourselves
but you with that motorised snap of a brain
still count the crocodile brother.

Then you did it.

For a day and a night this kingdom of ravens fell silent.
They're dropping their eggs from the sky
we said, which can only mean
death-line meridians roped round the earth
like so many nooses.
Whole cities in a single night.
Such big metal eggs you'd fashioned.

Crocodile like ourselves
only kills what he plans to eat.
We both lack ambition here, clearly.

Stealth bombers even borrow our plumage.

Of late we lost our appetite for anthropoid eyes
you having offered us so many.

Itinerary

Went to Ravenna one year
since our wings still flutter in its name.
Also tried Ravensbrück.
plus countless hills and hamlets
perched on the Yorkshire horizon
whose names acknowledge our black eyes
our claws, our sense of
the ultimate fitness of things.

You could navigate a zigzag
grand tour
mapped out entirely
from our species nomenclature.

Pruk says the Norseman
faced with sorrows of the weather
a daily sarcasm of winds
a wave's malevolence when mounted.
Pruk-pruk.
Often set to bleak
if haunting music
blown through a narwhal's tusk.
Such keening laments.

Vikings could never see
one of us ravens without promptly shooting.
Death thou shalt die, it would seem
by mere assassination of the shadow's emblem-man.

Ritual and Decorum

He wishes the nightingale would cut it out.
Blackbirds and robins are almost as bad.
The humming-bird's come-hitherish flutter
in a famous naturalist's hand
while cameras roll
makes him proud of his anthracite speech.

One song.
One note.
One colour.

As for variety
let seasons do our changing for us.

Only nested in this Tower
having mistook it for a small riverside mountain.
Utterly startled when you turned up down there
wearing such fancy plumage and waving your blades
preparing for the morning sacrifice.

Watched in silence
Anne Boleyn's head slice off.
Wondered if it might be coming our way
but regal decorum said no.

Four raw eggs every morning in the hall of the Mess.
The ritual that gets a day started.
If ever they're late
we push into the breakfast room of the yeomanry
to ask what's going on now in the world of men.

Whispering Gallery

We picked your words up
gleaning detritus
in this disused coalmine.
The decorations down here suit our mood.
Colliers' oaths and lamentations
ventriloquize our religion so precisely
a Davy Lamp stands on the altar of our cathedral
whose address I may never divulge
to any other species (particularly yours).
Its flame glows eternal.
Before that, as you may recall,
you'd use caged birds to test for firedamp.
Their ghosts fly round here still
tiny fluttering atoms in darkness
searching for the blackened hands
of kindly men who fed them once.